Dog Friendly
Tea Room & Café Walks

Wet Nose
Publishing Ltd

www.countrysidedogwalks.co.uk

First published in December 2015 by **Wet Nose Publishing Ltd**
All enquiries regarding sales telephone: 01824 704398
email cdw@wetnosepublishing.co.uk
www.countrysidedogwalks.co.uk
ISBN 978-0-9931923-2-6

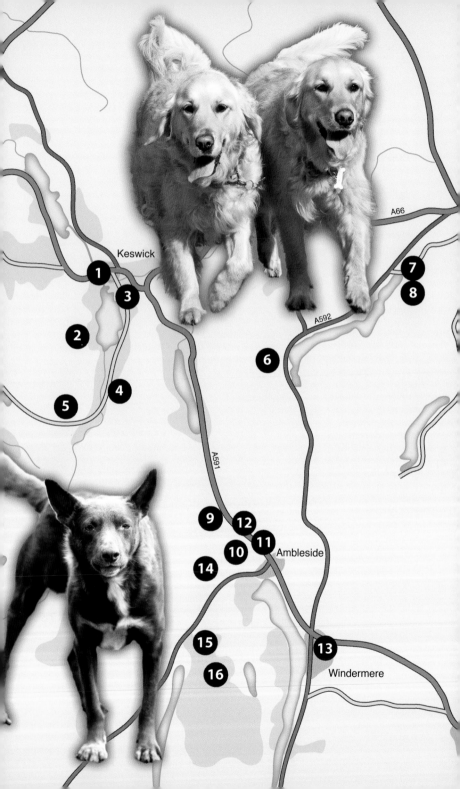

Contents

Introduction

The walks included in this book are all designed so that you and your wet nosed friend have a really enjoyable time. There are a few stiles, which have lift gates designed for dogs. At a quick glance there is information at the beginning of each walk to tell you what to expect and what you may need to take with you. The descriptive guides will also warn of any roads ahead or areas of livestock so that you can get your dog on the lead well in advance. Please be aware of deer throughout your walks, as they could be anywhere!

Dogs just love to explore new places. They really enjoy the new smells and carry themselves a little higher with the added excitement. Going to new places gets you and your dog out and about meeting new people and their dogs. It is important to socialise dogs, as they will be more likely to act in a friendly manner towards other dogs as they gain confidence.

The stunning pictures in this book are just a taster of what you can see along the way. Most of the walks are crammed with fantastic views and you are never far from water or woodlands the later will provide shade in the summer and shelter on cold, wet days where your dog will love the freedom to run up and down.

The walks are graded Easy, Medium and Challenging. They are all around one to three hours long, depending on your or your dog's pace. You may start with the easy ones and work up to the challenging walks depending on your and your dog's fitness. Different dog breeds and dog age must be taken into account when you decide which walks to do. If you are unsure of the distance that your dog can manage why not try the linear walks first. You will be able to judge if your dog is getting tired and so you can choose to turn back at any time. This is always good for older dogs, as some days are better than others and the linear walks are often flat making it easier to manage.

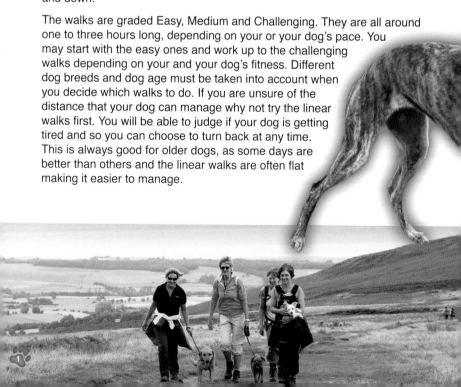

Different breeds of dog have different levels of fitness. For example bulldogs can only do short walks where as a border collie or a springer spaniel are extremely energetic and difficult to tire out. It is recommended that you research information on the breed of dog that you own to get to know what sort of exercise that they require.

You may have a walk that you are happy doing with your dog every day, but this book will show you new areas to explore with a change of scenery and a chance to meet new people and their dogs. Dogs love new places to visit and you will see the change in them as they explore the new surroundings, taking in the new smells with delight. You will fulfil your life and your dogs just by trying somewhere new.

There is plenty of water for your dog to enjoy, whether it be lakes, tarns, rivers or streams so for those dogs that love water you can be sure they won't stay dry for long. Some of the walks include bridleways, so you may encounter horses. It is important to put your dog on a lead if you see horses approach. It is always helpful to say hello to the riders as they near so that the horse realises that you are not a threat.

The Lake District National Park

The Lake District National Park was formed in 1951 to protect the beauty of the mountainous landscape and tranquil lakes from being developed into housing and industry. Most of the National Park is owned privately. Roughly 25% belongs to the National Trust and 3.9% belongs to the Lake District National Park Authority.

The villages and farmland only add to the beauty, which complement the natural landscape, with its heathlands, hedgerows and beautifully crafted stonewalls that are blanketed in moss and the quaint cottages and beautiful houses that have been built from local stone.

Ground Nesting Birds

Watch out for vulnerable ground nesting birds during 1st of March until the end of July. Dogs that stray off the main paths may disturb birds and chicks, possibly killing them or breaking eggs. Species to look out for are Sky larks, Meadow pipits, Curlew, Red and Black grouse, Snipe and Pheasants.

Some if not all of these birds are declining in numbers, due partly to their vulnerability when nesting. Dogs are a threat to them, even if treading on them unintentionally. Some other threats are foxes, badgers, stoats, weasels, birds of prey and crows.

Please help to protect these birds during the nesting season by keeping your dog on the paths when walking in open areas such as grassland, moors, heathland and scrub.

Rivers

Some dogs love water and will think nothing of plunging into the river. With the extreme weather conditions over the last few years a river that may be safe for your dog to swim in can change in a matter of hours, to become a swollen torrent that could wash your dog away. Please be careful when near rivers if there have been heavy periods of rain or if they look swollen or fast flowing. It is best to put them on the lead, until you have assessed the situation.

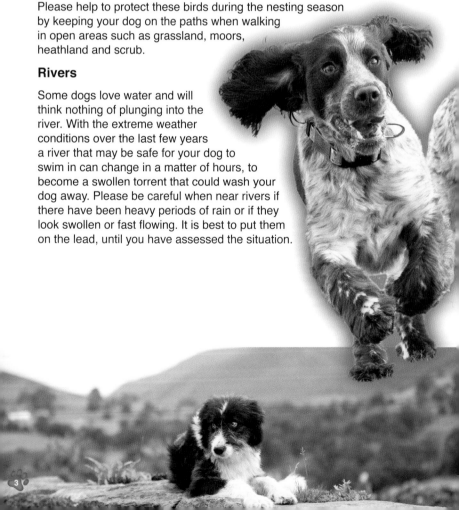

Forests

The forest walks in this book are a changing landscape, which makes them unique and interesting. Descriptions may change with time, for instance a path may be described as being in the shade of the forest, but as this is a worked forest a section could be clear felled at any time. Another change over the years could be where a view is described across a previously felled area. This could then be planted up and trees grown blocking the views. Paths may change but this is less likely. On rare occasions the Forestry Commission may temporarily close paths due to forest works but again this is even less likely on a weekend. Any changes to the path networks that may occur after the date of print will be updated on our website.

Does your dog fetch a stick?

Most dogs love sticks and will pick them up without any encouragement from their owners. Vets and dog trainers recommend that you should not throw sticks for dogs. It can cause nasty injuries, sometimes fatal as the stick can pierce the throat, or rebound off the ground and cause harm to your dog.

Ticks

If you have been walking in areas where sheep graze you should check your dog for ticks. They must be removed as soon as possible and best to use tick tweezers, which are specially designed to remove the head and leg parts of the tick. Ticks can carry diseases and the longer they remain latched on to your dog the more the chance of spreading infections.

Livestock

All walks avoid areas that cattle and horses graze. This can change however according to changes of farming with the individual landowner. If you find that you need to cross a field with cattle and they seem interested in you or your dog it is recommended to let your dog off the lead. Never try to get between cattle and your dog. Your dog will get out of a situation a lot easier with speed than you can. It is usually only cattle with young calves that can be a threat. Or young heifers or bullocks that tend to get a little inquisitive. They will usually stop when they get close to you or your dog.

If you encounter horses and they seem to get aggressive towards your dog, let the dog off the lead. Most horses will come over for a fuss but a small per cent do have a problem with dogs and will see them as a threat and will act to defend the herd. Horses that are out with a rider are completely different as they are not defending the herd and as long as you keep a safe distance there should not be a problem.

Sheep are not a danger to you but your dog can be a danger to them. Where sheep are grazing it is vital that you have your dog on a lead or under very close control. You will know your dog but if you are unsure better to play safe and keep your dog on a lead. It is important always to have your dog on a lead when around lambs. Lambs have a higher pitch bleat and are more cat size and your dog may act differently amongst them.

Please clean up after your dog

Always be prepared, having dog bags with you at all times. Once you have cleaned up after your dog, please keep the bag, until you see a bin. If there are no bins provided, then take it away with you to a roadside bin. Dog bags that are discarded on the paths or in the bushes are unpleasant and unsightly and will not degrade.

"I feel sorry for her too...but they won't let her in as she drips her wet coat all over the floor!"

1. Derwent Water   Challenging - 8.3 miles - 4hr 30min

This circular walk follows the edge of Derwent water, and although long it is fairly flat, except for a small hill through woodland towards the end. However the walk can be shortened to suit you, by getting the ferry (launch) across the lake. It is recommended if the water level is high to at least get the ferry to Ashness Gate (3 on map), to avoid a section of road, with only a narrow footpath. The walk can be halved by getting the ferry to High Brandelhow (5 on map). There are livestock on parts of the walk and there are some sections of road. The location of the cafe is indicated at point 6 on the map.

How to get there – From Keswick follow the sign for Borrowdale on the B5289. On leaving Keswick, look for the sign for Theatre/Lake car park.

Grid Reference – NY 261235

Postcode – CA12 5DJ

Parking – Pay and display Lakeside car park

Cafe – The Chalet tel: 01768 772757

You will need – Dog lead, dog bags

The Walk

❶ From the car park, continue to the toilet block. Pass this on your left and continue straight ahead, where you will veer around the back of the theatre. You will pass a metal sculpture on your right, and then you will reach an access road. Turn left and continue passed the front of the theatre on your left. This section can be busy.

Continue on the access road, where you will pass the jetty on your right (from the jetty you can get a ferry - known as 'The Launch', which will shorten your walk). Continue on the promenade. At the end of the promenade continue straight ahead on the quiet road. At the end of the tarmac road

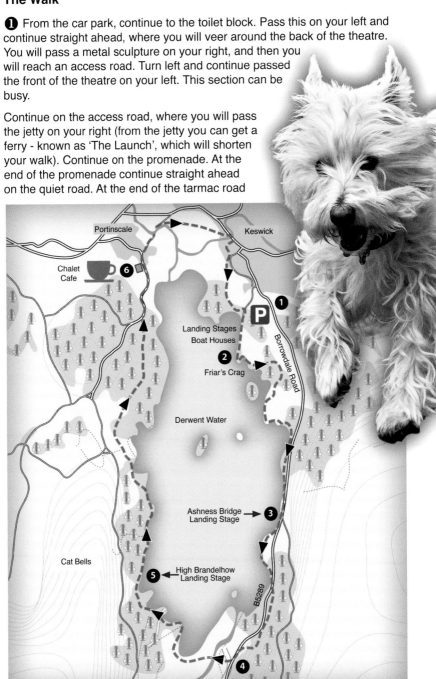

Portinscale

Keswick

Chalet Cafe **6**

P **❶**

Landing Stages
Boat Houses

2

Friar's Crag

Borrowdale Road

Derwent Water

Ashness Bridge
Landing Stage **3**

Cat Bells

High Brandelhow
Landing Stage **5**

B5289

4

you will reach a track straight ahead, signed Friar's Crag. Continue on this path and ascend for a short distance into woodland. **②** The lake is over on your right, below. Take a path on your left, signed for Strandshag Bay. You will pass a path on your right with steps, and then you will reach a gate. Put your dog on a lead, or under close control and pass through the gate. There may be livestock grazing here.

Continue on the path, beside the bank on your left, with the lake on your right. There are mature trees scattered throughout the area. Continue on the path, where you will pass over a couple of boardwalks. Pass through a gate and continue straight ahead into woodland carr (wet woodland) and wet meadows. Cross a footbridge over a beck and veer to your right. Continue on the well-made path. Pass through a gateway and turn right. Ascend to an access track, and keep your dog under close control and listen for any cars. Continue between the hedgerows, where you will reach a cattle grid straight ahead. Put your dog on a lead, or under close control and pass through the gate, beside the cattle grid. Livestock may be grazing here.

Ascend on the track, and on reaching a fork turn left. Continue on the track on the edge of grassland, beside a stock fence on your right. Ignore a kissing gate on your right and continue on the path. On reaching a gate, pass through it and take the path on your left. Continue beneath the yew trees. You will reach the lakeside once again. Continue on the path beside the stock fence on your left, with scrub on your right. Cross a footbridge over an inlet and continue beside the lake. Ignore a path on your left as you near a road, and keep your dog under close control or on a lead, as there are gaps in the stone wall beside the road. Continue straight ahead on the path beneath the trees.

Ignore any paths on your left, and descend for a short section, where you will put some distance between the road and yourself. Continue on the main path, and ignore any paths on your left. Cross a footbridge and turn right, where you will reach the lakeside once again. Continue beside the lake where you will pass a crag on your left.

High Water - If the water level is high you will reach the crag and you won't get around, this is soon after reaching the lakeside. If this happens you will need to go back to the footbridge, but don't cross it. Put your dog on a lead and turn right. Follow on the path, where you will reach the road. Turn right and continue beside the road, on the narrow path. You will reach the end of the path. For a short distance, continue on the road with care. On your right you will see a gap in the wall with steps. **③** Descend the steps to reach a jetty and turn left. Now follow the directions for low water.

Low Water - Continue with the lake on your right, where you will reach a jetty. Pass the jetty and continue, keeping your dog under close control or on a lead, as there is no wall beside the road ahead. The path will leave the road as you veer to your right. There is now a stock fence, with a field beyond on your left.

Cross a footbridge and continue on a path, which crosses a meadow. This meadow is quite floristic in spring and summer. After a while the path will reach beside the road once again. Keep your dog under close control or on a lead, as the wall has gaps. Put your dog on a lead and cross a footbridge into a car park. Go to the entrance of the car park and carefully cross the road. Take the path on the opposite side, keeping your dog on a lead or under close control, as there are gaps in the wall, where your dog can reach the road. Continue through the mixed broadleaved trees.

After a while you will ascend on the path, and you will veer away from the road for a short distance. There are many ferns and moss covered boulders on the woodland floor. The path undulates and you will continue beside the stone wall and road once again. Pass a sign for Mary Mount and continue. Just after you will reach a fork. Take the path on your left, and just after you will reach another fork. Again take the path on your left. You will reach and continue beside a stone wall, with a field beyond on your right.

Descend to the end of the stone wall, where you will reach another path and waymarker. For a short detour turn left and ascend, and veer to your right. You can enjoy the well-known Lowder falls. Continue back to the end of the stone wall and waymarker, and continue straight ahead. Put your dog on a lead and cross a footbridge over the river. Turn left and continue beside the Lowder hotel. Cross a small car park and continue on the drive, where you will reach the road. ❹ Cross the road and turn left. Pass a toilet block on your right and continue on the path beside the road. Descend for about 100m, and then take the path on your right. Pass through the gate, and keep your dog on a lead or under close control, as there may be livestock.

Continue on the well-made path through wet grassland. You will reach a wide river, cross the footbridge and continue on a boardwalk through the floristic wet meadows. Pass through a gate, keeping your dog under close control or on a lead, and continue straight ahead, beside the opposite end of Derwent water. The views are exceptional on a clear day, with fells surrounding the lake. Ascend on the path, between bracken, with mature scattered trees and rock outcrops. Cross another couple of boardwalks along this path to avoid the boggy sections. Pass amongst the trees and scrub with many rocks and crags.

Cross another boardwalk. You will then go through a gate into woodlands following the gravel path near to the lakeside. Pass over a series of small footbridges over streams. The path will weave in and out of sight of Derwent Water.

When you reach a house turn right on the quiet access track. Keep your dog under close control, and head towards another house. Pass through a kissing gate and follow the path, with the house on your left and a shed on your right. You will meet with the lake once more. Pass gorse on your left. Cross a footbridge over a stream.

Head for the gate along the water's edge, beside the shale bank. You will reach a copse of scots pines, where you veer to your left. You will meet two paths ahead. Take the lower path; pass a jetty and a couple of picnic benches. **❺**

Continue along this path with the lake on your right. Here there is beautiful mixed woodland, rock crags covered in moss, and many streams entering the lake. Cross a series of small footbridges where you will see pebble beaches.

You will pass a wooden carving of a pair of hands on your right. A little further on pass through a gate beside another jetty, and continue straight ahead, ignoring the path on your left. There is an open meadow on your left. The path bends sharply to your left as you continue around the top of a crag. Descend the crag and follow the grass path, beside a stock fence on your right. You will soon be on a more defined path. On reaching another path turn right.

Pass through a gate, keeping your dog on a lead or under close control and continue on the edge of a meadow. You will reach and pass through another gate. Continue on the path. After a while, pass through another gate and continue straight ahead, ignoring a narrow path which veers to your right. Pass a house over on your left and continue on the path, which ascends through a field. Pass through a gate and turn right on a quiet access path, keeping your dog under close control or on a lead. Continue beside the estate fence on your right.

On reaching another access road turn right. Pass a footpath on your right, which is signed for the jetty. Continue, where you will soon pass the driveway for Derwent Bay. Turn right after the driveway and pass through a gate into woodland. Continue on the path, with dense rhododendron and laurel. Descend and then cross a footbridge and go through the gate. Put your dog on a lead, or under close control as there may be sheep grazing. Pass through the middle of a boggy field on a well-made path. At the end of the meadow, go through a gate and continue on a path through the woods. Ascend gently beside a stock fence on your right. As you continue there are wire fences on both sides of the path.

You will soon have high deer fences on your right. At the end of this path, put your dog on a lead and pass through the gate. Just after turn right and continue beside the stone wall. You will descend on the path and there is a right hand bend. Here, continue straight ahead, following the waymarker. Continue through the mixed broadleaved woods ascending quite steeply. After a while you will begin to descend, quite steeply to a road. Turn right, where you will reach a pavement a little further along. Pass a marina, and then pass two entrances for the Dandelion Hotel. Cross the road to make use of the pavement on the other side. Pass Derwent water marina and continue. The pavement will run out, and you can cross to the other side to make use of a pavement. Soon after you will reach The Chalet on your left, where you can have a well deserved break. ➏

On leaving the café, cross the road and turn left. Pass beside Harney Peak and take the road on your right. Continue to the end of the road, ignore the footpath on your left and continue straight ahead. Cross the suspension bridge, where you will reach a dead end road. Continue on this road, but soon after go through the small gate on your right. Continue on the path, with a river on your right. Pass through the small gate and turn right. Continue on the well-made path, between stock fences, with fields on either side. The fells surround you in the distance.

Pass through a gate and continue between hedgerow and stock fence. Put your dog on a lead before reaching the end of the path. Pass through the gap and turn left. On reaching the main road turn right. Cross the road bridge, and then turn right on Bridge Terrace. At the end of the road ignore a path on your left and pass between the bollards. Continue straight ahead, and on reaching another road turn left.

Pass Booths supermarket and car park on your left, and on reaching another road turn right. You will join a path immediately after on the right hand side of the road. The path continues beside a quiet road. A little further on you will join the quiet road, where you will pass a rugby club on your right, and then the road becomes a lane. Pass three entrances into a caravan site on your right. At a sharp bend in the road, leave the road and go through the gate into Crow Park. Keep your dog under close control or on a lead and veer to your right and ascend. Continue on the level grass path near the edge of a sloped field.

You will soon see Derwent water ahead. Ignore a path on your right, just before the lake. Turn left on the edge of the lake, where you will have amazing views on a clear day, across the lake, which is surrounded by fantastically shaped fells. You will see another path, which veers to your left and leads to a gate. Take this path and on reaching the gate put your dog on a lead. You are now in a familiar spot. Turn left on the access path and continue to the car park.

2. Scope Beck Dam
Medium - 4.2 miles - 2hrs

This is a wonderful circular walk, where fells will surround you as you continue deeper into the valley. You will feel as though you are miles from anywhere and there are wonderful views, so you will need a clear day. You will cross many streams, where your dog can quench his thirst. There are boggy sections when you are near the end of the valley. There are some quiet roads, and livestock may be grazing throughout the walk. You will find the tea-room near to the end of the walk.

How to get there – From Keswick, take the A66 signed for Cockermouth. Turn left following the signs for Grange, Portinscale and Newlands Valley. Continue on this road, following for Grange and Newlands Valley. Continue following the sign for Newlands Valley. You will pass the Swinside Inn on your right. Continue on this road; turn left when you see the sign for Little Town. The sat nav will bring you to the edge of the village. Continue on a little further, and pass through the village. You will reach the car park just before going over a narrow road bridge.

Grid Reference – NY 231193   **Postcode** – CA12 5TU

Parking – Car park with an honesty box at Little Town

Cafe – Littletown Farm tel: 017687 78353

You will need – Dog lead, dog bags

The Walk

❶ Put your dog on a lead to begin this walk. From the car park, face the road and turn left. Cross the road bridge over the river. Take the quiet road on your left, signed Newlands. Pass Newlands school/church on your right. There is a river below on your right. You will leave the river, where the road bends to your left. There is woodland pasture on each side of the road, beyond the fences.

Ignore a footpath on your left and right and continue to ascend on the road. There is a small stream on your right at the side of the road, where your dog can get a drink. Ignore a footpath on your right. At the end of the road, continue on the driveway and pass a house on your right. Ascend on the path, and a little further on you will reach a gate. **❷** Keep your dog under close control or on a lead and pass through the gate. There are sheep beyond this point. Continue on the track, which cuts across a slope, with mature sycamore on your left to begin with.

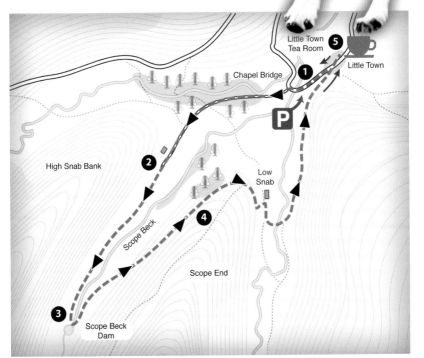

Ignore a small gate on your left, and pass through the gate straight ahead. Continue between stone walls to begin with, and then stay on the grass track between the bracken. You will be heading into the end of the valley between two fells. Hind Scarth fell is on your left and Robinson fell is on your right. Scope beck is the river which runs along the valley bottom.

You will pass beside some gorse on your right. Ahead you will see the man made dam, where the fells merge together. The track narrows as you reach nearer to the dam. Pass some exposed rock and a boulder on your right. You are closer to the beck here, and you can see the water as it rushes over the boulders. Ascend a little steeper and veer to your right as you reach the Juncus, growing on the boggy ground. The path fades away at this point, as walkers choose different routes to reach the dam and reservoir. Make your way to the dam and cross it, beside the small reservoir on your right.

❸ There are a couple of small waterfalls on your left. Cross the two footbridges and turn left.

Again the path isn't obvious as walkers choose their route through another boggy section and boulders. Continue on the same level and a little further along you will see the path once again. After you pass most of the boulders the path splits. Stay on the higher path, and soon after it will become unclear again as you reach another boggy area. Continue straight ahead, and soon you will see the path again. The path is narrow and little more than a sheep track, which cuts through the hillside.

As you reach back on dry land the slope on your right is covered in heather. As you continue there is heather/ling and bilberry on both sides of the path. The views are spectacular on a clear day, across the valley to the surrounding fells.

You will pass across a section of scree. As you continue the heather/ling is gone and you will have bracken dominating the area. You will see a wall below on your left. Pass a small outcrop on your right. You will reach an old mining area, with large exposed stone on your right, and a shaft on your left. Immediately after passing the shaft turn left. ❹ Descend the steep slope, passing the shaft on your left. At the end of the shaft turn right on a wider path. You will pass a small cave/shaft on your right soon after.

Cross over more scree, and then pass between boulders and continue straight ahead, where you will soon reach a stone wall on your left. Continue beside the stone wall on the track, which cuts through the hillside. You will veer away from the stone wall for a while. As you continue you will reach the stone wall again. Descend across some loose stone, taking care if you have your dog on a lead.

You will leave the fence line, and the path will level out. Descend a little further, turning left just before reaching a concrete block and post and rail fence. Descend to a fingerpost and turn right following the sign for Dalehead. Continue on the wide track heading into another valley end. Cross a stream, leave the track and turn left, following the sign for Dalehead and Little Town. Cross a small stream on reaching a stone wall. Pass through a gate and descend to the footbridge. Providing the river isn't flowing too quickly, your dog can cool off here.

Cross the footbridge over the river and continue beside the stone wall on your left. On reaching a wide track turn left. Ascend gently beside a stone wall on your left. Fells surround you in all directions here, making for stunning scenery. As you continue you will see the church/school, which you passed on your outbound route and the car park below on your left. Look behind here to see the stunning shapes of the fells. The triangular shaped fell is Scope End.

Ignore a path on your left and continue to ascend on the track. On reaching a gate pass through it and descend to the road. Turn right (straight ahead) on the road. ❺ You will find 'Little Town Tea Room' on your left. On leaving the tea room turn right on the road and descend back to the car park.

TEA ROOM + BAR
OPEN 11am – 5pm
HOT + COLD DRINKS
DRAUGHT BEER + LAGER
HOMEMADE CAKES,
SCONES + SANDWICHES
ICE CREAMS

3. Walla Crag

Medium - 3.5 miles - 2hrs

This circular walk has a very steep descent, and can be very challenging if you have your dog on a lead. There are some sheer drops on the edge close to the steep descent, but this section of the walk has a wonderful alpine feel. There is a river below and you descend amongst pines, and pass some crags and boulders. It is an amazing walk, with wonderful scenery and fantastic views. There is an ascent through forest and open ground, which is a little steep. Your dog will enjoy the wonderful woodland, heathland and scrub. There are livestock on parts of the walk, but there are no roads. Your dog will find water from the many streams along the way. The café is reached a quarter of the way around the walk.

How to get there – From Keswick, follow the signs for Buttermere on the B5289. With Derwent Water on your right, you will pass a National Trust yard on your left, and a little further along the road the National Trust car park will be on your left hand side.

Grid Reference – NY 272214

Parking – Great Wood National Trust car park pay and display

Cafe – Annie's Pantry tel: 07816 824253

You will need – Dog lead, dog bags

The Walk

1 From the car park, take the narrow path opposite the ticket dispenser. Ascend passed a picnic bench and continue through the mixed woodland. Cross a stream via the stones, where your dog can get a drink. On reaching another path turn right, and continue to ascend on the track. Ignore a track on your left, and continue straight ahead. On reaching a fork, take the path on your right and continue to ascend. The path gets a little steeper as you continue.

A couple of streams pass under the path, where your dog can cool off. Ignore a grass path on your right and ascend steeply. Just after, you will reach another path where you turn left. Descend on the path and cross another stream. Ascend again, a little further. You will leave the cover of trees, where you will have views across Derwent water, Keswick and Bassenthwaite. Descend between a stock fence and a stone wall.

2 On reaching another path and fingerpost turn left, following the sign for Keswick. Continue on the path, and soon after you will pass a mast on your left.

You will have farmland on your left, and a wooded slope on your right with the river below. Descend quite steeply on the path. Descend between stone walls and turn left. Continue to descend on the stone path through woodland. Pass through a gate. Continue straight ahead, where you will reach the café - Annie's Pantry. ❸ You can enjoy a rest, before you continue on your walk.

On leaving the café turn left and pass through the gate. Retrace your steps, ascending on the path. When you reach the fingerpost and a path on your right from your outbound route continue straight ahead, following the sign for Castlerigg/Walla crag. Pass through a kissing gate and keep your dog under close control or on a lead, as there may be sheep grazing. Continue on the path, which is undulating. The path widens and you will reach and cross a footbridge over the river. Continue straight ahead, through an open, scrubby area. Put your dog on a lead, pass through a kissing gate, and on reaching a quiet road turn right.

Continue on the road, until you reach another footbridge. ❹ Cross the footbridge and continue on the path. Ascend beside the stone wall on your right. Ignore a track on your left and continue to ascend quite steeply. You will reach and pass through a gate. Keep your dog under close control, or put him on a lead, as there may be livestock in the area. Continue to ascend on the path beside the stock fence on your left. You can stop and get your breath back and turn around to enjoy the views. As you continue, follow the stone wall on your right. You will ascend on the steep path, where the views on

your right will extend as you continue. You will reach a level section of the path. You can see Derwent water, Keswick and Bassenthwaite. Latrigg is the small mound on the right of Keswick, and Skiddaw is behind Latrigg.

Continue on the path, where you will reach a cairn (pile of stones). Here, go through the kissing gate on your right. Continue straight ahead, ascending between the heather. The path becomes undulating, and the scenery is superb here, especially when the heather is in flower. The views on your right are breath-taking on a clear day. Descend on the path, which cuts through the hillside and pass over exposed stone in places.

A little further along, you will descend into silver birch trees. Cross a stream and then ascend over exposed rock. Continue on the path and ascend to a small crag/outcrop. There are views in all directions, and it's a wonderful place to stop on a clear day and take it all in. ❺ This is the highest point of your walk. Continue over the crag and descend on the worn path between grasses, bilberry and ling. There are scattered silver birch and rowan trees. You will reach a stile on your left, now you need to have close control of your dog, or put him on a lead. Cross the stile, using the lift gate for your dog and turn right.

Ignore the path on your left, and continue straight ahead between the bracken. You will see Derwent water straight ahead. Take a path which forks to your right and continue to descend, beside a stone wall. Descend quite steeply now. Pass through a gate and continue beside the stone wall. Ignore a path on your right. You will reach steep steps. You need to be extra careful if you have your dog on a lead. Descend the steps and then descend on exposed rock. There is a makeshift hand rail to help. Keep your dog under very close control, or on a lead, as there are sudden drops into Cat gill on your left in places.

The path zig zags, and you leave the stone wall. Pass through a kissing gate and descend beside coniferous trees. Descend a set of steps between a stone wall and a stock fence. Pass through a kissing gate and continue to descend amongst boulders, with a stone wall on your right. You will reach a gate, where before going through your dog can get access to the gill. Go through the gate and continue to descend beside the stone wall, through the mixed woodland. Mosses and ferns carpet the floor. You will leave the stone wall on your right and continue on the edge of the woods. Ignore a path on your left with a footbridge (it is worth crossing, just to enjoy looking over into Cat gill). Continue to descend straight ahead. You will leave the gill behind and the path now is quite tame.

You will enter into the woods. Ignore a path on your right, and pass beside a vehicle barrier. Ignore a path on your left, and continue straight ahead. You will soon reach back into the car park.

4. Watendlath Tarn

Medium - 3.2 miles - 2hrs

To enjoy this quaint tea garden you will need a pleasant dry day, as there is no indoor seating. A clear day is well recommended to appreciate the amazing scenery in all directions. This circular walk is very peaceful and you will enjoy the rugged landscape, crossing open heath and moors, with scattered boulders and crags. The walk can be boggy in places. There is water all the way for dogs to get a drink and a cool off. There are livestock throughout the walk. The tea garden is located at the beginning/end of your walk.

How to get there – From Keswick take the B5289 in the direction of Borrowdale. After approximately two miles turn left, following the sign for Ashness Bridge and Watendlath. Continue on this narrow one-track road until you reach the end, where you will find the National Trust car park.

Grid Reference – NY 275163

Postcode – CA12 5UW

Parking – Pay and display

Cafe – Caffle House Tea Garden. Due to being situated in a remote area the opening hours vary. The Tea Garden may not be open on a bad day weatherwise. Seasonal.

You will need – Dog lead, dog bags

The Walk

❶ From the car park, go back to the entrance and continue on the quiet road. Pass a footpath on your right and a house on your left. On reaching another road at the end of a stone barn on your left, turn left. The tea garden is on your left. Turn right and cross the bridge over a stream.

Turn left and head towards the tarn. Pass through a kissing gate just as you reach the tarn, and continue on the path. On reaching a fingerpost take the path signed to Dock Tarn. Pass through a gate and continue on the path between stone walls. Cross a small stream and ascend a little on the path, which cuts across the hillside.

Pass through another gate beside a stone stile. Keep your dog under close control or on a lead as there is livestock grazing in the area. You will continue beside a stream on your left. Cross another stream and then turn sharply to your right. Follow on the track ascending gently. The track will become unclear; keep close to the stone wall on your right. At the end of the stone wall cross a stream and turn right, following the waymarker. You will have a stream on your right once again.

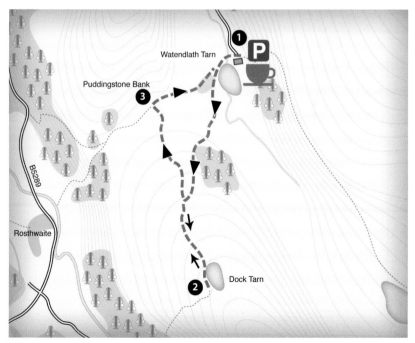

Ascend a little steeper. Cross the stream and continue to ascend beside the stone wall on your right. Pass through a kissing gate and turn left. Continue to ascend on the well-worn path between bracken. On reaching a sign, turn left for Dock Tarn. Cross the small stream and continue on the stepping stones over wet grassland. There are crags on your left.

You will reach another stream as you turn a bend. Continue beside the stream and cross it soon after. Pass through a kissing gate. Ascend now quite steeply, following the stone block path, which is more like a steep stairway. Stop for a breather, and turn to look at the views.

As you reach a crag on your right, there are some higher steps beside the crag. As you ascend you will reach some heather, which looks lovely when it's in flower. After some distance you will reach a crag straight ahead. Here there is a left and right path. Take the path on your left and cross over another small stream. There is a steep slope on your left, covered in heather/ling. You will soon see the tarn ahead of you. The view of the tarn will come and go. The path is rocky and un-even in places. On reaching the tarn, the path continues around one side. You can go to the end of the tarn if you wish, but this is the furthest point to your walk. ❷

When you are ready, simply turn around and retrace your steps. You will enjoy new views on your return. After passing over the wetland section via the stones, look for a sign on your left for Puddingstone Bank and Rosthwaite (just as you cross the small stream and before turning right on your outbound route). Continue straight ahead following the sign for Puddingstone Bank.

Continue on the worn grass path. There are some posts which mark the route, as the path can be a little un-defined. Cross a stream and then you will cross a section which is boggy. On reaching a stone wall pass through a kissing gate and continue straight ahead through open grassland. Again the area is boggy and the path is un-clear, as walkers have chosen different routes to avoid the wet areas. After crossing the boggy section, ascend a little way. Descend then, where you will reach a stone wall. Pass through the gate.

Continue straight ahead and cross a boggy section. You will reach a wide well-made path. Look to your left here where you will have views into the valley, which is surrounded by fells. ❸ Turn right on the path. The path crosses over a stream and as you continue it becomes a little rugged as you reach a tree line. Descend beside a stock fence on your right. The path becomes sunken, with a bracken bank on your left. A familiar house and tarn will come into view. The path will merge with your outbound route.

Pass through a kissing gate and then cross the bridge. Continue straight ahead, where you will reach the tea garden. From the tea garden there is a gate into the car park.

5. Johnny Wood

Easy - 1.7 miles - 1hr 30min

This is a lovely circular walk, with the café midway along. You will pass through wonderful broadleaved woodland and lightly grazed sloped grassland. There is a wonderful river, where your dog can have a splash about, if the water is flowing steadily. There are two short sections of easy scrambling over rock, where care should be taken if you have your dog on a lead. Sections of the walk will have livestock grazing.

How to get there – From Keswick, follow the sign for Borrowdale on the B5289. Continue on this road for about 7.5 miles. Further along the road, follow the sign for Honister Pass and slate mines. On reaching Seatoller you will find the car park on your right hand side of the road.

Grid Reference – NY 245139

Postcode – CA12 5XQ

Parking – Pay and display National Trust car park

Cafe – Youth Hostel Cafe tel: 017687 77257

You will need – Dog lead, dog bags

The Walk

❶ With your back to the entrance to the car park, face the toilet block and turn right. On reaching the far corner of the car park, ascend on the path between the stock fence and stone wall. You will see fells in the distance on your right. Put you dog on a lead, or under close control, as there may be livestock. Pass through the gate and continue to ascend. Just after veer to your left, and continue on the grass path between the bracken.

Ascend gently. Cross a stream, where your dog can get a drink, and as the bracken thins out there are mature widely spaced trees. Ascend to a gate, put your dog on a lead or under close control and go through it. Cross another small stream and then take the track which veers to your left. The ascent is a little steep, and you will reach and pass through another gate into oak woods.

Continue on a level path, which cuts across the wooded hillside. Ascend again through a bracken dominated woodland clearing. The path levels out again as you go back into the woods. There

Longthwaite

Jonny Wood

High Doat

2

3

Seatoller

P

❶

B5289

are many shades of green, with moss covered boulders, ferns and grasses on the woodland floor. Continue on the well-worn path. You will begin to descend gradually and on reaching a stone wall, pass through the gap.

Descend steeply now, and then turn a sharp left bend at the edge of a steep wooded slope. There is a short section of easy scramble, as you cross over exposed stone. At the end of the slope go through the gate and turn right. Continue in the woods, with a stock fence on your right. As the trees clear on your left there are views across to the wonderfully sculptured fells. You will pass farm buildings on your left, and then shortly after you will reach a gate. Put your dog on a lead, as there are livestock and pass through the gate.

Turn left and continue to the access track. Turn right, and just after you will pass a car park on your left and a camping area on your right. ❷ You will reach the café on your right shortly after, where you can enjoy tea and cake. On leaving the café turn right. Continue on this access road to the end of the youth hostel. Continue on a path, beside the river amongst broadleaved trees. Pass through a kissing gate and continue on the worn path.

❸ The river is stunning here, with boulders and pools. The path is rocky as you pass over sections of exposed bedrock. The path is a little precarious as you cross beside a small crag. You will turn sharply to your right, where you leave the river behind. Continue on the path with the wooded slope on your right and a stone wall on your left, with a field beyond it. Ascend gently on the path. Keep your dog under close control or on a lead and pass through a kissing gate and continue to ascend gently between the bracken, where you pass through an opening in the trees.

Ahead you can see more rounded fells. Ignore a minor path on your left and continue straight ahead. You will glimpse the river below on your far left. Over on your left you will see a moss covered stone wall. A little further on you will reach the stone wall, where you pass through a gap. Turn right onto another path and continue through the woods, with a stone wall over on your right.

On reaching another stone wall pass through the gap. Continue on the well made path. Pass the end of a stone wall on your left. Ignore a kissing gate on your right and continue straight ahead. There are moss covered boulders scattered around the landscape. Ascend to a kissing gate and pass through it. Turn left and continue on a path at the foot of a slope, which is dominated by bracken. You will reach a familiar gate. Pass through the gate and descend back to the car park.

6. Glenridding

Medium - 3.3 miles - 2hrs 30min

This is a fabulous circular walk, which has wonderful views across Ullswater and the surrounding fells. You will feel very much at peace on this walk, as you get off the beaten track and enter into wonderful scenery in the heart of the valley. A steady climb brings you deeper into the valley, but you will be above and looking down into it. There are streams and Glenridding beck, where your dog can cool off and get a drink. There are livestock throughout the walk, and there is a quiet road at the beginning and end of the walk. The café is located near to the end of your walk.

How to get there – Take the A592 from Windermere towards Penrith, and on reaching the village of Glenridding you will find the car park on your left off the main road.

Grid Reference – NY 385169

Postcode – CA11 0PD

Parking – Pay and display

Cafe – Helvellyn Country Kitchen tel: 01768 482598

You will need – Dog leads, dog bags

The Walk

1 From the car park, continue to the furthest end from the road on the higher level. As you enter the higher level go to your right, where you will see a path. Continue between the stone walls, where you will pass a health centre on your left. On reaching the road turn left. Ascend on the residential road. Pass the Travellers Rest on your right, near the top of the road.

As the road bends sharply to your right, leave the road and continue straight ahead, following the sign for Glenridding Bridge. Shortly after you will descend on the road. Cross a bridge and ascend again. Take the path which veers to your right, and continue beside a stone wall, with the road on your left. The track soon ascends with Mires beck on your left below. As you reach a fingerpost turn right, following the sign for Greenside Road. Keep your dog on a lead, or under close control, as there may be livestock.

Pass through the gate and ascend on the track which cuts across the hillside. You will soon reach a stock fence on your right. There is a steep wooded slope on the other side of the fence. After you have passed the stock fence and trees, there is a field on your right which drops away. Continue to a gate and pass through the small gate. Veer to your right on the obvious track. On reaching a stone wall, pass the wall and veer to your right, following the waymarker. Pass through a small gate and cross

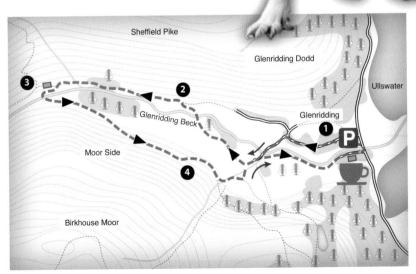

36

a footbridge over Glenridding beck. Check the flow, before letting your dog have access to the beck.

This is a beautiful spot in the valley, where you are surrounded by fells. Continue straight ahead and ascend the steps. Pass through a kissing gate and continue on the path, beside the stone wall. You will leave the wall and ascend between bracken. On reaching a stone wall on your right, pass through the small gate and turn left. ❷ On reaching a concrete track, turn left. Keep your dog under close control, as this is an access track for vehicles.

Ascend more gradually, beside a stone wall on your left and a bracken bank on your right. The track will level out. Continue along the valley. Ascend a little more. You will pass a stone hut and a copse of pines on your right. At the end of the track put your dog on a lead, as you will pass a house on your left. There is a small stream on your right, where your dog can get a drink. Pass a youth hostel on your left. After the car park, cross a bridge and go through a kissing gate.

Continue between buildings and follow on the track taking a sharp right hand turn. You will pass the disused Greenside mine. Turn left just after and continue to ascend. Ignore the track on your right and continue straight ahead, following the sign for Red Tarn and Helvellyn. Keep your dog on a lead, as there is a drop over a weir ahead. Pass the old mine workings on your right. Continue to ascend and pass the weir on your left. Just after cross a footbridge, where you will see a small waterfall. ❸ Turn left and head back along the opposite side of the valley. Keep your dog under close control or on a lead, as there will be sheep grazing.

Dog Friendly Tea Room & Café Walks - Lake District

The path crosses some exposed rock and cuts across a steep sided slope. As you turn a bend, there are wonderful views of Ullswater and the surrounding fells. There is a line of crags above on your right. As you continue you will pass between bracken. Ignore a grass path on your left. The path narrows and is undulating. Cross a footbridge where your dog can get water from the stream. Just after, cross another footbridge. Pass a rock outcrop on your right. A little further on you will pass an outcrop on your left.

❹ Just after this, veer left and descend the loose rock and stone, taking care if you have your dog on a lead. The path becomes grass, and you will descend a little steeply. You will reach a stone wall and another path. Turn right on the path and continue between the bracken.

Descend gradually, and on reaching a gate pass through it and descend beside a stone wall on your left on a cobble stone path. A stream crosses under the path, where your dog can get a drink. On reaching another path turn left and descend, with Myers beck on your right. Pass through a gate (which is often open) and ignore a path on your left, which was your outbound route. Continue to descend on a familiar path. On reaching the road take the first right turn (before crossing the bridge) and follow the sign 'Path to car park'. Continue on the track, with a stock fence on your right and a beck on your left.

Continue beside a campsite on your right. There are mature trees on both sides of the beck. After you pass the campsite you will enter into a small copse of trees. Just after, turn left on another path and continue with the beck on your left. The track will lead to a road. Put your dog on a lead and continue. You will pass beside houses. You will soon reach Helvellyn Country Kitchen on your right, where you can enjoy a well-earned rest.

On leaving the café turn right and on reaching the main road turn left, and cross the road bridge. You will reach the car park on your left.

Dog Friendly Tea Room & Café Walks - Lake District

7. Pooley Bridge Easy

1.5 miles - 1hr 30min

This circular walk starts with the River Emont, where your dog can enjoy a splash in the water. It continues through farmland to reach Dunmallard Hill, which is an ancient settlement. The hill is wooded, and you will walk around the outer edge. There are some stiles, but there are dog lift gates. You will pass through a section of farmland, where there will be livestock grazing. There is a short section of road at the end, where you will reach the tea-room.

How to get there – From Penrith take the A66 towards Keswick. At the Rheged roundabout take the A592 following the sign for Ullswater. Turn left onto the B5320. The car park will be located on the left hand side of the road, just before going over the road bridge.

Grid Reference – NY 46956 24450

Postcode – CA11 0LL

Parking – Pay and display

Cafe – Granny Dowbekin's tel: 07887 672385

You will need – Dog lead, dog bags

The Walk

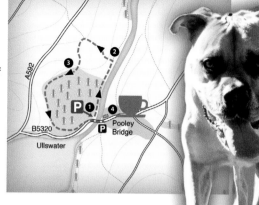

❶ From the car park take the bridleway at the furthest end of the car park. Before you let your dog off the lead check the flow of the river. Continue on the edge of the woods with the River Emont on your right. You will reach a beach area, where your dog can enjoy the water, if it's safe. The path ascends a little and you will reach a gate. Put your dog on a lead, or under close control, as there may be livestock. Pass through the gate, leaving the woods behind. Continue straight ahead, on the edge of a hilly field. Alder and willow trees offer shade along the river bank.

❷ Before you reach the end of the field (about 50m) turn left on the grass track at the edge of the hill. Ascend slightly, and keep the tree line on your left. You will see the gate ahead and on your right. Pass through the gate into another field, where there may be livestock. Turn left and continue on the field edge, with a stock fence on your left. There are mature oaks along the fence line. Ignore a stile on your left and continue a little further. You will reach another stile on your left. Cross this, using the lift gate for dogs.

Continue ahead and left (left of the telegraph pole) and cross the field. There are views in all directions. You will reach and cross another stile, with a lift gate. Continue straight ahead, but a little to your left ascending across the field. Head for the field corner and the woods. On reaching the corner of the field pass through the gate. **❸** Turn right on the path. Ignore a couple of narrow paths on your left just after. Turn right and descend on the path. Stay on the woodland edge, where ferns blanket the ground.

The path undulates and you will have views across farmland on your right, where the trees allow. As you continue, you will see Ullswater straight ahead. You will continue near to a stock fence on your right. A little further along, descend on the path. Ignore a path on your right and continue to descend. Ignore another path on your right and continue straight ahead. After a level section you will descend again and the path will reach close to the boundary fence and busy road. Keep your dog under close control or on a lead, to ensure he doesn't breach the fence onto the road.

Where the path splits, take the path on your right, staying beside the road. You will reach a gate on your right. Put your dog on a lead, pass through the gate and pass the car park on your left. Cross the road bridge, taking care as there is no pavement. After you have crossed the bridge you will find the tea-room on your left. **❹** The food is wonderful and is all cooked and baked on the premises. On leaving the tea-room turn right and cross the bridge back to the car park.

8. Pooley Bridge Chall.   6.5 miles - 3hrs 30min

This is a wonderful circular walk, and on a clear day there are many fantastic views along the way. The walk has several ascents, but they are not too steep. You will walk through open areas of grassland and moor, where sheep graze. There are some fields to cross and there is a small section across boggy ground. Pass through a camp site, where you will reach Ullswater, where your dog can enjoy a swim and cool off. There is a section of road without a pavement. The café can be reached three quarters of the way into the walk. Your dog will find water in many places along the way.

How to get there – From Penrith take the A66 towards Keswick. At the Rheged roundabout take the A592 following the sign for Ullswater. Turn left onto the B5320 where you will reach the village. Continue through the village and turn right immediately after passing St Pauls Church, which is signposted for Howtown. At the cross roads continue straight ahead. Continue on this quiet road, where you will reach a lay-by on your left near the end of the lane.

Grid Reference – NY 47865 23627   **Postcode** – CA10 2LT

Parking – Free in the lay-by

Cafe – Granny Dowbekin's tel: 07887 672385

You will need – Dog lead, dog bags

The Walk

1 From the lay-by continue to ascend to the end of the quiet road. Pass through the gate straight ahead of you, keeping your dog on a lead or under close control, as there may be livestock. Ascend on the track, with views on your right. The area is open hilly ground, which is dominated by bracken in places. Ignore any grass paths on your left and right. Continue on the wide path ascending through the open area. There is a gully on your left, where your dog can find water in places.

On reaching a cairn (pile of rocks) turn right. There are views in all directions. Continue on a fairly level path across Divock Moor. Several streams cross over and under the path as you continue, where your dog can get a drink. There is some heather and cotton grass amongst the grasses. You will reach a stone circle on your left. The path turns sharply to your right here. **2** As the lake comes back into view, ignore a grass path on your left. The path will narrow for a short section, and then you will join another wider path, which comes in from your right.

Continue on the wide path where you will reach a wide stream (Aik Beck). Cross this via the stones. Turn immediately to your right and ascend to a stone wall.

Turn left here and continue beside the stone wall on your right. You will descend gently, and there are views ahead and to your right to the many fells in the distance. Streams will cross the path in places and there is a gully on your left, which has running water in places.

As you continue you will have more views of Ullswater, surrounded by many shaped fells, which is breath-taking on a clear day. There are fells above on your left. Descend for quite a distance on this path, which cuts across the hillside amongst the bracken, grasses, scattered boulders and trees. You will reach and continue beside a woodland block on your right.

You will pass a stone barn on your right and then you will continue beside a stone wall on your right. A little further along look for a gate on your right, which has a waymarker on it. Put your dog on a lead, as there is a house ahead. Pass through this gate. ❸ Continue on the path, which veers to your left beside a stone wall on your right. Descend to a farmhouse. Pass through a gate and cross the front of the house. Pass through another gate and continue on the farm track, through the field, veering to your right. Pass through a gate and descend beside the stone wall on your left. Before the path bends to your left and reaches another gateway, turn right and follow the sign for Thwaitehill. Continue between stock fences and then pass through a gate.

Continue on the edge of a field, beside the stone wall on your right. Pass between the gorse scrub and cross a stream. You will veer away from the stone wall and cross through the field. Follow the worn grass path. It can be boggy here. Pass over another stream and continue between the gorse, beneath a line of telegraph wires. You will reach and continue beside a stone wall on your left. At the wall corner you will reach a gate. Go through the gate and continue beside the stone wall on the edge of a small field. Pass a house on your left.

Cross over a stream and go through the gate. Continue straight ahead, between barns and sheds. Pass through a small gate on your right, and turn left immediately. Continue straight ahead on reaching a track. As well as sheep, there are free range hens in this area, so remember to keep your dog under close control or on a lead. Continue straight ahead, ascending the track through the middle of the field. Ignore a path on your right and continue straight ahead. Pass a house on your right and continue straight ahead, where you will reach a stream and then a gate. Pass through the gate and cross another stream, via boulders. Cross the field veering to your left slightly. You will reach and walk beside a stone wall on your left. At the corner of the field pass through a gate. Turn right and continue beside a stone wall on your right on the edge of another field. Continue around the corner of the filed and then pass through a gate.

Turn second right on a farm track. Pass through a gate and continue between the stone walls. Pass The Chalet on your right and just after you will reach a

tarmac track. Put your dog on a lead and turn left. Descend between the stone wall and hedgerow. On reaching a road turn right. There are no pavements, so listen for cars, and take care. Ullswater is on your left. Continue on this road for about 500 meters. You will pass a house on your left and immediately after (before reaching the stone barns) turn left. ❹ Keep your dog on a lead and pass the house on your left and turn right on the drive.

Pass the Waterside House campsite facilities and continue on the concrete track. Pass a play area on your left and a barn on your right. Stay on the track nearest to the lake. Continue through the campsite and ignore a path on your right. Pass through a kissing gate, if the main gate is closed. Immediately after veer to your left and pass through a gate, beside an interpretation panel for Hodgson Hill. Continue on a path, beside the lake with the campsite on your right. At the end of the path, you will reach another gate. Put your dog on a lead and go through the gate. Turn left and continue beside the lake on the edge of the campsite.

Cross a bridge, pass through a gate and continue on the edge of the lake, with wet meadows on your right. Cross another footbridge and continue beside the water. You will reach and continue over a boardwalk near to the edge of the wet meadow. At the end of the boardwalk, pass through the gate and continue beside a stock fence on your right, with the lake on your left.

As you continue you will reach and walk between fences. Cross a wooden footbridge over Aik Beck, which you crossed higher up on the moor. Continue straight ahead and pass through a gate. Continue beside the lake, between the trees. If the water level is high there is a path above the bank on your right. Pass a tall wooden barn on your right, slate walls on your left, and then pass the jetty on your left. Put your dog on a lead, as there are houses and a road ahead. Continue on the path, beside a hedgerow on your right.

At the end of the path, pass through a gate and turn left on an access road. At the end of the access road, cross the main road and enter into the tea-room on the opposite side. ❺

On leaving the tea-room, cross over the road. Turn left and continue through the village. Immediately after passing St Paul's Church take the road on your right, which is signposted for Howtown.

At the end of the road cross over and continue straight ahead, following the sign for Hill Croft. There is no pavement on this quiet road. Ascend gently and ignore a road on your left, which is the entrance for Hill Croft caravan park. Continue straight ahead, and ascend a little steeper. As you continue you will have views across to Ullswater and the surrounding fells on your right. Go passed a track on your right and soon you will reach back to where you have parked your car.

9. Grasmere & Alcock Tarn Easy/Chall 1.6 / 4.2 miles

This circular walk is challenging, however you can do a section of the walk, which would make it an easy walk. After walking through part of the village, continue beside the river. You will cross through fields and then a main road, before you begin to ascend the fell to the lovely tarn. This is a lovely spot, with wonderful views and a peaceful place for a picnic. There are some quiet roads, which have no pavements, and you will need to cross a busy road if you choose the challenging route. You are advised to do this walk on a good day, as it is quite exposed. There are livestock on the short and long walk. You reach the cafe near the end of the walk (indicated with blue arrow on the map).

How to get there – From Ambleside take the A591 towards Keswick and follow the signs for Grasmere. Turn onto the B5287 and pass the first car park on your right. On reaching the village turn left, following the sign for car park.

Grid Reference – NY 338077

Postcode – LA22 9SW

Parking – Pay and display

Cafe – Heidi's Cafe tel: 015394 35248

You will need – Dog leads, dog bags

The Walk

❶ From the car park go out onto the road and turn right, taking care, as there are no pavements. Ignore the road on your left just after leaving the car park. On reaching another road cross over and turn left. Pass St Oswald's cemetery on your right, and then pass Wordsworth Daffodil Garden. Immediately after you pass the garden turn right onto the riverside path. Continue between the fences, with a meadow on your left and trees on your right. A little further along you will reach and continue beside the river. Check the river flow, before allowing your dog into the water.

Further along the path there are views ahead and to your left of the fells, Black and White Knotts and Butter Crag. There is a spot where your dog can reach the river a little further along, providing it isn't too fast a flow. You will reach a footbridge on your right. **❷** Cross the footbridge, and then on reaching the path turn left. Put your dog on a lead or under close control and pass through the kissing gate. There may be livestock in the fields.

Continue on the path, on the edge of pasture land, close to the fence on your left. After you pass an old stone fence post on your right continue straight ahead and cross the corner of the field. There are views to the surrounding fells in all directions. Pass

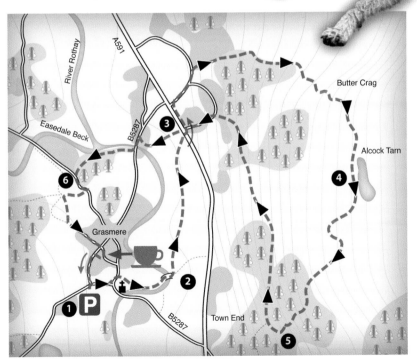

through a kissing gate and continue through another field. Cross diagonally to your right slightly, and head towards the gate. Pass through another kissing gate and cross another field. Continue straight ahead and head for the field corner, and another kissing gate.

Pass through the kissing gate, turn left and follow the worn path on the edge of the field. Pass through a farm gate in the field corner. There is a busy road ahead. Put your dog on a lead and continue between the fence and the stone wall. Continue to the farm gate. Pass through the gate onto a pavement beside a busy road. ❸ Turn left.

The Challenging Walk - 2hr 30min

Cross the road at the crossing island. Turn left and continue on the pavement. Turn right on reaching a quiet road, beside the Swan Hotel on your left. Ascend the road, which has no pavement. Ignore a road on your right. There are wonderful views on your left. Shortly after turn right where you see the fingerpost signed for Greenhead Gill and Alcock Tarn.

Ascend on the narrow road between the stone walls, and after passing the stone wall on your right you will continue beside the lovely river. Ascend quite steeply here. At the end of the road continue straight ahead and go through the gate. Turn right and cross the footbridge over Greenhead Gill. Continue on the worn path beside the gill, with a stone wall on your right. There are large rock boulders scattered in the landscape.

Continue beside the stone wall and veer to your right, leaving the gill behind. Ascend steeply on the stone cobble path. The path will leave the stone wall as you veer to your left. The path gets steeper again. There is a stone wall on your right, hidden from bracken in places. Look behind, catch your breath and enjoy the view. You will leave the stone wall behind at a dog leg in the path, which snakes through the hillside. The path widens and is grassy. Veer sharply right, where the path is narrow once again. Veer sharp left as you see another stone wall. Continue to ascend steeply, where you will have views on your right across Grasmere to the fells beyond. The area opens up as you ascend out of the bracken. Veer right and continue on the path. You will reach near to a stream on your left, where your dog can get a drink. Pass between crags on your far left and right. Pass some more crags on your right and then pass beside a stone wall on your right, after crossing over a small crag. Continue on the path and pass through a gate.

You will now reach the tarn. ❹ Continue beside the tarn on the well-worn path. This is a great place to stop, enjoy the views and rest for a while. After you pass the stone wall on your right the views are incredible on a clear day. Pass the tarn and continue on the wide grass path. There are views of Windermere ahead. Veer to your right and pass through a gap in the stone wall, where you will start your descent.

Follow the worn path which snakes around the steeper sections. Cross some

exposed stone beside rock crags. You will descend between the bracken again. Pass over a stream. As you descend you will have views across Grasmere. On reaching a stone wall pass through a gate and continue on the path. Pass another rock crag and continue on the path. The path zigzags around a steeper section of the fell.

Pass a pond on your left and then you will reach larch and oak trees. On reaching a waymarker follow the white arrow, taking the path on your right. **5** Descend to a kissing gate. Pass through the gate and continue on the worn grass path. Continue straight ahead and pass mature trees on the path, which cuts across the hillside. Cross a footbridge over a stream and as the bracken clears there is a stone wall on your left.

Cross a stile, which has a lift gate for dogs. Leave the stone wall and continue about 20 yards and then veer left and descend on a narrow path amongst trees. Cross a small stream as you leave the cover of trees. Continue beside the stone wall on our left. The bracken closes in on your right. Cross another stream and shortly after pass through a kissing gate. Continue straight ahead, passing through the wildly spaced mature trees and then between bracken and trees. Continue beside the stock fence on your left and then a stone wall. At the end of the stone wall put your dog on a lead and turn left. Pass through a gate and continue beside the stone wall. Pass Grasmere Lodge on your right and go through another gate onto a quiet road.

Continue straight ahead on the road, which has no pavement. You will reach a main road. Cross this at the familiar island. Turn left, and just after take the footpath on your right. Now follow the directions for the short walk, but ignore the first sentence.

The Short walk - 1hr

Take the footpath on your left (just before you reach a traffic island). Continue between the stone wall and a stock fence. As you pass between old stone gateposts put your dog on a lead, as there is a road ahead. At the end of the path turn right and continue on the access path, beside houses. On reaching a road turn left. Cross a road bridge and then cross the road and go through the gate opposite, into Butharlyp Howe wood. Continue straight ahead.

Ascend beneath the trees, with a river below on your right. As you continue, the river below will veer off to your right. There is a low boundary wall ahead, so keep your dog under close control or on a lead. You will pass a house on your right and then you will reach a gate. Put your dog on a lead and go through the gate, with care and turn left on the road, **6** which has no pavement. Pass Glenthorne guest house on your right, and then take the second gate, which is signed by a fingerpost (seen above the wall) for

Langdale. Pass through the gate, keeping your dog on a lead, or under close control, as there may be livestock grazing.

Continue beside a fence on your right, on the edge of pasture land. At the end of the second house on your right, turn left onto a gravel path. On reaching an entrance road turn left. Go to your right of the gateway, where you will pass through a gate, to avoid the cattle grid. Continue on the road. On reaching another road, cross the head of another road on your right and continue carefully on the main road, as there are no pavements. Pass the Red Lion hotel on your right. You will reach Heidi's café on the right hand side of the road, where you can enjoy a hot drink and a bite to eat.

On leaving the café, turn left on the road and immediately left again. Follow the winding road beside the cottages. On reaching another road turn left, and at the end of the road, you will reach the car park.

10. Lily Tarn

Challenging - 3.5 miles - 2hr

This circular walk crosses through fabulous scenery, where you will gain wonderful views, after a steep ascent on a quiet access road. You will cross many streams and walk beside a river. You will be surrounded by fells and crags as you continue through open lightly grazed grassland. Lily tarn is a wonderful, peaceful place to stop, where your dog can take a dip in the water. On your descent there are spectacular views across Ambleside and to the surrounding fells. There are livestock on this walk and a couple of quiet lanes. The cafe is located near the end of the walk.

How to get there – Ambleside is north of Windermere on the A591. Continue through the village, around a one-way system. Shortly after leaving the one-way system continue straight ahead over the roundabout, following signs for Keswick. You will pass over a road bridge, and the main car park will be found immediately afterwards on your left.

Grid Reference – NY 37416 04788

Postcode – LA22 9AY

Parking – Pay and Display

Cafe – The Apple Pie Cafe tel: 015394 33679

You will need – Dog lead, dog bags

The Walk

1 Leave the car park from the main entrance and cross the bride and turn left on the road. Pass the police/ambulance station and turn left on Stoney Lane. At the end of the road take the footpath on your right, signed Miller Bridge. Follow on the tarmac path beside a metal fence with the river beyond on your left. There is a stone wall on your right. The path bends to your right, away from the river. Continue between the stone slab walls.

As you continue there is a stock fence on your right, with fields beyond and trees and scrub on your left. At the end of the path, put you dog on a lead and pass through the gate. Cross the lovely stone bridge over the River Rothay. You will reach a quite road, where you turn right. Pass through a gate beside a cattle grid and ascend gently on the quiet road. Just after, pass between old stone gateposts and then turn left on the public bridleway. **2** Ascend quite steeply on the access road.   There are woods on both sides of the road. Again there are stone slab walls on your left. There is a stream below on your right.

Your dog can find water from a stream on your left just before it goes under the road. Pass a couple of houses on your left and continue to ascend on the road. As you reach a sharp left bend in the road you will pass more houses on your left. **3** The road now is reduced to a track. Ignore the footpath on

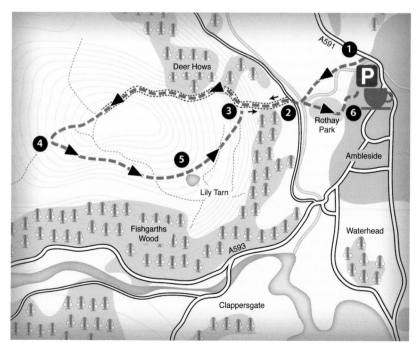

your left and continue on the track. There is beautiful woodland on both sides of the track, beyond the stock fences. Ignore a gate on your left, and then a footpath on your right. Continue straight ahead, between stone walls.

On reaching a gate straight ahead put your dog on a lead or under close control, as there may be livestock. Pass through the gate. Continue beside the stone wall on your right, with grassland and bracken on your left. Pass a stream, where your dog can get a drink. The stream will be close to the path on your left. Continue to ascend a little. Pass Pine Rigg on your right. Just after, pass through the gate straight ahead. Continue on the path, beside the stone wall on your right, through open hilly grassland.

There are views on your right to the fells beyond. The path veers to your left, away from the stone wall. There is a small stream on your right. The scenery is wonderful, with hills, rock outcrops, trees and in the distance fells surround you. Continue straight ahead and pass through another gate, signed for Loughrigg. Stay on the well made path in the open hilly area, which is dominated by bracken. As you continue a little further you will begin to descend. Cross a stream via the boulders and continue straight ahead. After about 50m you will see an unmarked path on your left. ❹ Take this path and descend between the bracken.

Cross a stream via the stones. You will pass briefly beside a stone wall on your right. Ascend again on the path. There is exposed stone amongst the bracken. Ignore an unmarked path on your left and continue straight ahead. Soon after, descend and cross over a small rocky section. You will reach close to a stone wall on your right. Continue straight ahead and pass through a kissing gate. Ascend straight ahead, beside the stone wall on your right. Continue over bedrock beside a stone wall on your right. As you leave the stone wall the area opens up, with wonderful views over Windermere on your right. Ignore an unmarked path on your right and continue straight ahead. There are views in all directions. Pass some small pools on your left. You will descend and then reach Lily Tarn. ❺ This is a beautiful place to stop, and there is a bench. Pass the bench and at the end of the tarn turn left.

Descend between the bracken. The path can get a little boggy. Pass a small pool on your left and continue straight ahead on the grass path between the bracken. Just before you reach a stone wall, you will have views over Ambleside. Descend to the wall and pass through the kissing gate. Descend the wide grass path between bracken and enjoy the wonderful views. The path bends to your left and then almost immediately it will bend to your right. Ignore the track on your left. You will reach close to the stone wall on your left, where you will hear a stream.

The path is boggy as it bends to your right. Cross over bedrock for a short section. Ignore an unmarked path on your right. Descend the steps and then cross the footbridge. Enter into woods and continue beside a stock fence on

your left. At the end of the path pass through the stone wall and descend the steps. You are at a familiar spot. Turn right on the road, and descend. At the end of the road turn right. Cross the bridge on your left and then turn right. Cross another bridge and turn left. Follow on a tarmac path, where you can enjoy the river beyond the metal fence on your left.

There is a woodland copse growing over the rock outcrop on your right. Keep your dog on the path before you reach the football pitch. Continue around the pitch and put your dog on the lead before the end of the path. At the end of the path turn left. Pass beside the church on your right. Continue on the quiet road. At the end of the road turn left and continue to the end. On reaching another road turn left. **❻** The Apple Pie Café will be on your left a little further on. On leaving the café turn left and then left again. Pass between shops where you will then reach the car park.

11. Ambleside Waterfall Med - 1.4miles - 1hr 30min

This walk is partly linear with a loop in the woods, where you will see the wonderful waterfall. There is a footbridge, where you can cross over the top of the waterfall, which is a fabulous experience. There is some road walking, and at the beginning and end the road is busy as you go through the village. The café and tea rooms are located near to the beginning/end of the walk. There are no livestock on this walk.

How to get there – Ambleside is north of Windermere on the A591. Continue through the village, around a one-way system. Shortly after leaving the one-way system continue straight ahead over the roundabout, following the sign for Keswick. You will pass over a road bridge, and the main car park will be found immediately afterwards on your left.

Grid Reference – NY 37416 04788

Postcode – LA22 9AY

Parking – Pay and Display

Cafe – Spoilt for choice: Bilbo's Cafe, The Rattle Gill and the Giggling Goose

You will need – Dog lead, dog bags

The Walk

❶ From the car park go back onto the road and turn right. Continue beside the main road. Cross over the road and continue beside the shops on the main high street. Pass North Road on your left and then take the narrow road on your left, which is signposted for the toilets.

❷ This road has no pavement. Pass the toilets on your right and then pass Cheapside on your right (there is a dog friendly café here called Bilbo's). Continue around a left hand bend, where you will see a sign for the waterfall. Ascend gently and pass a parking bay on your right. A little further on, you will see a river on your left. The road will get a little steeper as you continue. Pass another layby on your right. You will see another sign for the waterfalls. **❸** Take the path on your left. Enter into Stockghyll wood, and keep your dog on a lead, as the river flow is rapid at this point. Continue on the path beside the river, and follow the red arrows.

Turn right and ascend the steps. Ignore the steps on your left and continue on the path. A stream passes under the path, where your dog can get a drink on your right. On reaching a fork turn right and then ascend on the path through the mixed broadleaved wood. There are steps in places. As you ascend there are some viewing areas on your left where you can see the waterfall. Continue to ascend a set of steps, where you will reach the larger area to view the waterfall, which is truly stunning.

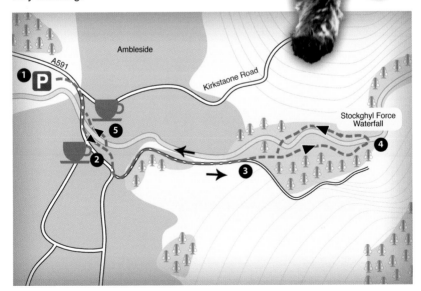

Continue following the waymarkers, turn left and ascend the steps. Cross slate slab bridges over streams, where your dog can get a drink. Ascend the steps and turn left. Pass a picnic bench and you will then reach a stone wall. Turn left and cross over a footbridge at the top of the waterfall. ❹ This is a wonderful experience, where you can see and hear the water flowing rapidly over the rocks below.

Turn left and continue on the main path, with the river on your left below. Descend a set of steps and then continue beside a metal fence on your left. You will descend to another footbridge. Cross the bridge over the river and continue on the footpath. Cross a stream and ascend the steps. You are now at a familiar spot.

Take the path on your right and retrace your steps beside the river. On reaching the quiet road turn right. Descend on the road, veering to your right just before reaching the toilet block. Turn right on reaching the main road. Turn right again onto North Road. ❺ There is a choice of two cafes; the first one is The Rattle Gill. To locate this café, turn left on Bridge Street, which is a narrow back lane. The second café is the Giggling Goose, which is located just after Bridge Street on your left, just as you cross the road bridge.

After leaving Rattle Gill café, turn left and continue on the back lane, where you will reach the main road. If you have visited the Giggling Goose, you can get to the main road via the tea garden. On reaching the main road turn right and cross the road, where you will soon reach the car park.

"At least we shake our coats properly!"

Dog Friendly Tea Room & Café Walks - Lake District

12. Rydal Beck

Easy - 1.2mile - 1hr 30min

This is a short circular walk, however it is a little steep in places. You will reach and walk beside the beck. As you begin to ascend you will continue beside the stunning waterfalls. The area here is delightful, with many shades of green, from the trees to the mosses, which cover the boulders. You will pass through a wonderful oak wood. The tea room starts and ends near to where you park your car; therefore you can enjoy the delicious refreshments before or after your walk.

How to get there – From Ambleside take the A591 towards Grasmere and turn left following the sign for Rydal Hall.

Grid Reference – NY 349065

Postcode – LA22 9LX

Parking – On the roadside, before the entrance into Rydal Hall

Cafe – The Old School Room Tea Shop tel: 015394 32050

You will need – Leads, dog bags

The Walk

1 Enter Rydal Hall via the second entrance, where you will see a fingerpost signed for Ambleside. Ascend on the access track, keeping your dog on a lead or under close control. You will pass two paths on your left. On reaching the end of the building on your right, you will have a building straight ahead of you. This is the tea room. Turn left here; pass the picnic benches on your right and a building on your left. Turn left and continue on the narrow path, beside the beck below on your right, and the building on your left.

Pass a game larder on your right and continue on the path, ascending gradually through the mixed broadleaved wood. The beck passes over boulders in places, creating the lovely sound of rapidly flowing water.

2 You will reach and cross a footbridge over the beck. Ascend on the path, which veers away from the beck for a little while. The path becomes a little steeper. Pass a deeply cut channel on your left. Look out for a narrow path on your left. Keep your dog under close control or on a lead, as there are sudden drops in places and take this path where you will enjoy views of the beck in the gorge below. Ignore the steps on

your left, which lead to a disused bridge. You will pass wonderful waterfalls as you continue. There are some steps in places as you ascend on the path, amongst the mass of greenery - ferns, mosses and trees. Even the boulders are covered in green mosses and lichens.

You will reach level with the beck, where your dog can have a dip. Continue on the path, which will veer away from the beck. You will reach a track (which you left earlier). Continue straight ahead as you join onto it. There are mature oak trees on both sides of the track. Continue to ascend, and you will see the beck again on your left. You will ascend a little steeper, and on reaching a level you can see a weir on your left. The water generates electricity here for the hall below. ❸

Take a narrow path on your right here, which is waymarked. Continue to ascend into the mixed broadleaved wood. You will reach close to a stone wall on your left. A little further on veer to your right, following the waymarked route. The path and the arrows can be obscured by bracken in the summer months. The path will become more obvious again as the bracken thins a little. There are boulders scattered here and there.

Descend a little further and look out for an obvious grass path on your right, which isn't currently marked. Take this path and descend gradually through the wood. You will reach a wide track. Turn left on this track and continue to descend. The track will be a little steeper as you continue. There are small pools on your left, which attract wildlife. You will soon reach a familiar spot on the track. Ignore the path on your right, which is the path to the waterfall and continue on the track.

Take the next path on your right (from your outbound route) and descend, where you will cross the footbridge again. For a short detour of five yards, continue ahead and right, and have a look at the 'Ice House' on your left. Go back to the path and turn right to continue your outbound route beside the beck. You will reach the tea room, where you can enjoy wonderful cake and a hot drink, if you haven't already been in! There are other delightful paths in the hall's gardens, which you can explore before going back to your car, but you will need to keep your dog on a lead.

Old school room
Tea shop
Dogs and muddy boots
Welcome
OPEN from 10.00am daily
Rydal Hall
Come on in
we're
OPEN

13. Orrest Head

Medium - 4.2 miles - 2hr 30min

Please note there is a stone stile on this walk, which is easy on entering, but the ground is lower on the other side and there are steps. This will be fine for dogs that can jump down off a low wall. For dogs that can't manage this, owners have the option of making this walk a linear. Both the circular and the linear walks pass through wonderful woodland. You will ascend steadily, and on reaching the top, you will be rewarded by wonderful panoramic views across Windermere to the surrounding fells. The circular continues through oak dominated woodland and you will cross a field, where cattle and sheep may be grazing. There are no livestock if you choose the linear route. There are roads on this walk at the beginning and end, as you pass through part of Windermere. The café can be found near the beginning and end of the walk.

How to get there – On reaching Windermere on the A591, turn onto Main road or High Street (both roads will continue onto Crescent Road, which is a one way street). Just after leaving the one-way street turn left onto Broad Street, which is signposted for the car park. The car park will be on your right hand side.

Grid Reference – SD 413982   **Postcode** – LA23 2AB

Parking – Pay and Display Ellerthwaite Square Broad Street

Cafe – Coffee Bar 7 tel: 01539 446584

You will need – Dog lead, dog bags and water for your dog

The Walk

❶ Leave the car park on Ellerthwaite Square (entrance to the car park) and turn left. Continue to the main road, and turn right. Continue on Crescent Road, which is a one way street. Stay on this road, beside the shops (you will pass the cafe on Oak street on your right). It will become a two way road again. Continue straight ahead, and just after turn right onto High Street. Ascend to the top of the road and turn left. Cross the main road using the pelican crossing. **❷** Turn right, and then just after the metal railings on your left, turn left. Here, follow the sign for Orrest Head on the quiet access road.

There is no pavement here. Take the footpath on your left, which is marked with a fingerpost. Follow the sign for Troutbeck Road. Continue between the stone wall and the hedgerow. The path will widen. Continue beside gardens on your right. You will soon ascend with woodland on your right, which has many rock outcrops.

On reaching a fingerpost, turn right and follow the sign for Orrest Head. Cross a small stream

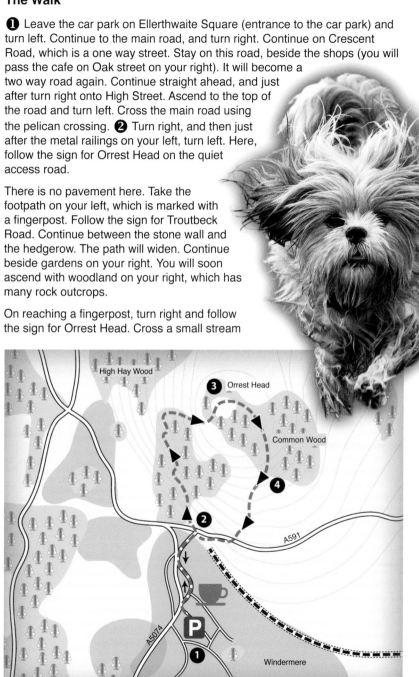

where your dog can get a drink. Continue to ascend between the stone walls, which are blanketed in moss. You will reach another path. Turn left (or straight ahead as you merge onto the path), and continue to ascend with a stone wall on your left. There is woodland on both sides. On reaching a stone wall straight ahead, turn left. Follow the waymarker for Orrest Head. On reaching a gate and a stone wall, turn right and ascend some steps beside the stone wall.

Ignore any paths on your right. Continue straight ahead on the edge of the wood. There is a lot of bedrock as you ascend. You will leave the wood and continue straight ahead, now with a stock fence on your right and sloped fields and trees. As you continue there are views on your right across Windermere. You will reach the end of the path. Go through a kissing gate on your left. Continue straight ahead, beside a stone wall on your left. Ascend the steps between the trees. The path will get a little steeper. You will reach some exposed stone; continue over this, where you will reach the view point at Orrest Head. ❸ On a clear day the views are fantastic, over Windermere and the distant fells which surround it.

This is the furthest point of the walk if you want to avoid the stone stile and the possibility of livestock. If you want to continue follow the directions under the heading Circular walk.

Linear walk

Simply turn around and retrace your steps back. On reaching the main road, cross at the pelican crossing and then turn left. Cross the road again, where you see the tourist information on the opposite side. Turn right on this road. Now follow the directions under the heading – Both routes merge here.

Circular walk

From the concrete slab bench, face the views and take the path on your left on the edge of the hillside. Descend slightly on the grass path, with the views on your right, and bracken on your left. You will reach the trees and soon after a stone wall. Turn left and continue beside the stone wall on your right. Bracken and scattered trees are on your left.

Descend on the path. You will reach a squeeze stile (there are steps or a jump from the other side). If your dog can't mange this stile then simply turn around and retrace your steps and follow the directions for the linear walk.

Continue over the squeeze stile and turn right. Pass through the kissing gate and continue on the edge of the woods. There are views on your left. The path

is beside a stone wall to begin with. Cross over a small section of bedrock and into woods. Descend on the obvious path through the mixed broadleaved wood. Stay on the path and cross stepping stones over a wet area as you go through an opening in the stone wall. Continue straight ahead and follow the fingerpost sign for Windermere. Ascend gently on the path through the wood. On reaching a gate, put your dog on a lead or under close control and go through the gate. **4** There may be livestock in the field. Continue straight ahead beside the stone wall on your right. There are sloped fields on your left. Descend and pass briefly between the stone walls, and then go through a small gate. Turn right and put your dog on a lead. There's a busy road ahead.

Continue on the path between the stone walls. Pass a gate on your left and then pass a gate on your right. Pass through the gate straight ahead, where you will reach a busy road. Cross with care, and then turn right. Descend beside the road. Cross the road, where you will pass the sign for Windermere railway station on your left. Turn right and pass the tourist information. Continue on the pavement and turn left.

Both routes merge here.

Continue on this road, which veers left into a one way street. Turn left on reaching Oak Street, where you will find Coffee Bar 7 on your left.

On leaving the café turn right and then almost immediately turn left and continue on the one way street. Turn left on Ellerthwaite Square (Broad Street), where you will reach back to the car park.

 Dog Friendly Tea Room & Café Walks - Lake District

"Don't look now darling but the mongrels from next door are coming over to our table!"

14. Ivy Crag

Medium or Chall. - 2miles - 2hr 30min

This circular walk is a medium, but there is an option to extend the walk and make it a challenging one. If you choose the longer walk there is a steep ascent and a short scramble (20ft), which is no more than a rough steep stairway. There is stunning scenery, where you will be surrounded by fells. There are wonderful views on both walks and you will pass beside Loughrigg tarn. There are livestock throughout this walk and some quiet country lanes. There is also a very brief spell along a busy road, but there is a footpath. There is plenty of water along the way for your dog. The café will be reached near to the end of your walk.

How to get there – From Ambleside take the A593 to Clappersgate, and then follow the signs for Elterwater on the B5343. Just after entering onto the B5343 you will find parking on your left, close to the Talbot Bar.

Grid Reference – NY33977 04327

Postcode – LA22 9NJ

Parking – On the left of the roadside after the Talbot Bar on the B5343

Cafe – Chester's By The River tel: 015394 34711

You will need – Dog lead, dog bags

The Walk

❶ Put your dog on the lead to begin this walk. Cross over the road opposite the entrance to the Talbot Bar car park. Go through the kissing gate and keep your dog on a lead or under very close control as livestock may be grazing. Continue straight ahead following the sign for Loughrigg Tarn,   and cross through the field, beside a stone wall on your right.

Continue straight ahead at the end of the stone wall and ascend across the middle of the field. You will reach another stone wall, and then pass through a gate. Continue to ascend between a metal fence and a stone wall. There is an avenue of mature trees. The path narrows where you veer to your right. On reaching the end of the stone wall, go through the gate on your right. Put your dog on a lead, as you will pass through a holiday village.

Continue on the stone path between post and rail fence through a beech wood. Pass between wooden cabins to reach a tarmac drive. Continue straight ahead and follow the waymarkers. Cross an access road and ascend on the road straight ahead. Continue ascending on this road, ignoring any roads to your left or right. On reaching the end of the sealed road continue straight ahead, where you will pass through a small parking area.

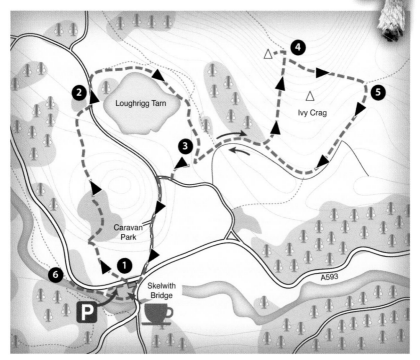

Continue straight ahead, ignoring any paths on your left. You will reach a stone wall. Pass through the gate, where you will have views on your right and ahead across the beautiful sculptured fells. Continue straight ahead on the well-worn path between bracken. As you continue, and just before you begin to descend you will see Loughrigg Tarn on your right.

Descend between the bracken. You will reach a stone wall on your right. Keep your dog under close control, as there is an access track ahead. Continue beside the stone wall. On reaching the access track put your dog on a lead, as there are free range hens and a road ahead. Continue straight ahead, with a stone wall on your right. Pass a cottage and a stone barn on your left. ❷ On reaching a road turn left. Descend the quiet road and look for a stile on your right. Cross the stile, using the lift gate for your dog. Keep your dog on a lead or under close control, as there may be livestock.

Continue on the well-worn path across the field, but just before reaching the ladder stile veer to your left and pass through the gate. Cross a stream via stones and veer to your right towards the tarn. Continue on the well-worn grass path beside the tarn on your right. There are mature ash and alder, which provide pleasant shade on hot days, and your dog can cool off in the water.

You will veer away from the tarn and the path will become a little less obvious. Cross a leet and continue to cross the field straight ahead, towards a stile and estate fencing. Cross the stile using the lift gate and turn right. Continue on the track between estate fencing. You will pass a campsite and a house on your right, and then go through a gate. Put your dog back on the lead.

Long Walk

❸ Take the path on your left, which is signed for Ambleside. Pass through the gate and continue between the stone walls. Cross a small stream where your dog can get a drink. Ascend on the path and ignore the footpath on your left. There are fields on both sides beyond the walls. As you ascend you will pass a small conifer plantation on your left. Pass through another gate and continue to ascend beside the stone wall on your right, and a bracken bank on your left. Cross a small stream and then immediately turn left on an unmarked path (if you reach a tall gate on your right you have missed your turn).

Ascend the bracken bank on the narrow path, which is quite steep. You will turn sharply to your right, leaving the stream and pass a small crag. You will cross the stream a little higher up. Continue to ascend between the bracken. Stop and catch your breath, taking in the views from behind you. You will see a stone wall over to your left. As you continue on the path you will reach the stone wall and continue with it on your left. You will pass a rocky crag on your left. On reaching another wider path it is worth a little detour to ascend the crag, to reach the highest point of the walk. ❹ The views are outstanding

from the top on a clear day. You will view Loughrigg tarn and surrounding fells. Go back to the wide path and turn right. You will soon descend on the well-worn path. Ignore any narrow paths on your right. There are wonderful views ahead. Ignore a path on your left and continue straight ahead. There is a short scramble, where you descend a rock crag. Continue on the path and pass a pond on your right, where your dog can cool down. Just after you will reach another path just before a stream, and turn right. ❺

Continue straight ahead, where you will enjoy views amongst the wonderful scenery. Descend on the well made path. Pass another stream. You will reach and continue beside a stone wall on your left. There are good views across Windermere on your left. Ignore a path on your right. Pass a tall gate on your left and continue. You will cross a familiar stream and continue on a familiar path. On reaching another path and Tarn Foot Lodge, follow the directions for the short walk (the first path to ignore on your left is the path you have just been on).

Short Walk

Ignore the path on your left (for the long walk), and then on reaching a fork immediately ahead turn right towards another house. Pass a row of cottages on your right and then turn left at the road junction. On reaching another fork, turn right along the quiet road. Shortly after you will reach a road on your left, turn left onto this road. Pass a parking bay on your left and a river. Continue descending the road and pass another house on your left. Continue to descend. The gradient will steepen and you will reach a very busy road ahead.

On reaching the main road don't go first right, but go right along the main road. Head towards the Skelwith Bridge sign and follow on the pavement/track along the main road. Pass the Skelwith hotel, and then turn right as you see the sign for Chester's by the River. Pass the cottages on your right and enter into Chester's Café. After you have had your well-earned rest, and you have left the Café turn left and cross the shop front. On reaching an access road turn left. Pass the old mill buildings. Stay on this path with the river on your left. It is best to keep your dog on the lead, as there is a gap in the wall ahead, which leads to a road. Pass a path and fingerpost on your right.

Keep your dog on the lead and descend the steps on your left to view the magnificent waterfall. ❻ When you are ready cross the bridge, ascend the steps and turn right on the path. Shortly after, take the path on your left beside the fingerpost, which goes to the road. Before reaching the road take the path on your right, between the trees. On reaching the road, turn right and continue on the narrow path beside the road, where you will reach back to your car.

15. Coniston

Medium - 4.3 miles - 2hr 30min

This is a wonderful circular walk. You will pass through fantastic countryside with sloping hills and views to the fells and Coniston water. There are forest plantations, woodland, and streams along the way where your dog can get a drink. You will walk beside a river, where your dog can cool off. There are livestock for parts of this walk and some roads as you walk through the village. The cafe is located at the halfway point of the walk.

How to get there – Take the A593 from Ambleside towards Coniston. Tom Gill car park will be on the left hand side a good distance before reaching Coniston.

Grid Reference – SD 321998

Parking – National Trust Pay and Display

Cafe – Hollands Cafe tel: 015394 41303

You will need – Dog leads, dog bags

Dog Friendly Tea Room & Café Walks - Lake District

The Walk

❶ From the car park, continue straight ahead with your back to the road. At the end of the car park ignore the track on your right and ascend on the track straight ahead. There is a stream on your right, where your dog can get a drink. You will pass a farm gate on your left. Continue between stone walls. You will reach a farm gate straight ahead. Put your dog on a lead or under close control as there may be livestock grazing, and there is a quiet road ahead. Pass through the gate. **❷**

Continue on the path, with a stone wall on your right and a grass/bracken bank on your left. There are mature oak and ash trees on the bank. As you reach a road ahead turn right and go through the kissing gate, keep your dog on a lead or under close control, as there are livestock. Continue on the driveway for Tarn Hows Cottage. There are views on your right to near and distant fells.

On reaching a sharp bend on the tarmac path, just before the house, leave the path and pass through the small gate, signed Permissive Route. There are no livestock on this section of the walk. Descend beside a stock fence on your right. Continue between the bracken on the obvious path. Ignore a gate on your right and descend gently amongst the trees. You will reach and continue beside a stone wall on your right.

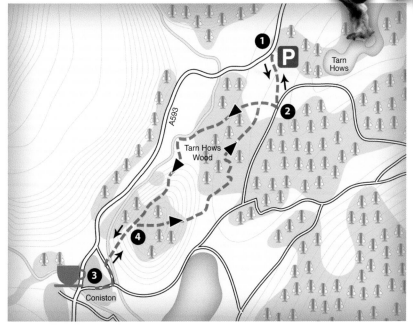

After veering away from the stone wall continue to descend through the hilly woodland. A stream passes over the path, where your dog can get a drink. Ignore a grass track on your left and continue on the stone path. The path becomes enclosed with young silver birch trees. Cross a footbridge over a stream and continue through the woods. You will reach a river on your right on the woodland edge. Check the flow of water, before letting your dog have access to it.

Continue beside the river, and soon you will reach a kissing gate. There are views of Yewdale fell straight ahead. Keep your dog on a lead or under close control, as there may be livestock, and pass through the kissing gate. Continue on the edge of the field beside a stock fence on your right. You will reach and pass through another kissing gate. Turn left on the track. following the sign for Coniston. There is a hedgerow on your left and a river on your right. If the flow of the river is gentle, your dog can access at a couple of points where there are steps.

After a sharp right hand bend you will see a fingerpost and a kissing gate on your right. Keep your dog on a lead or under close control. Pass through the kissing gate, following the sign for Coniston. Cross the field straight ahead on the worn grass path. There are views to the fells on your right, beyond the sloping field. Continue to a stone wall and then pass through the kissing gate. Remember to keep your dog on a lead, or under close control, as livestock may be present. Continue on the obvious worn path, which will bend sharply to your left after passing a mature oak tree. Pass a second oak tree just after, and then turn right. There is a stone wall a little over to your left. You will pass a waymarker on your right and then ascend across the hilly field, with scattered mature trees. The path veers away from the stone wall. Continue into the trees where the path becomes more defined.

On reaching another stone wall pass through the gate. There are no livestock for the next section of this walk. Continue through the plantation. At the end of the plantation pass through a kissing gate. There may be livestock so keep your dog under close control or on a lead. Pass under a line of yew trees and continue straight ahead, descending on the path between the bracken and gorse. There are views ahead over Coniston and to the hills beyond. Coniston water is on your left and there are fells on your right.

Another path joins the path you are on, from your left (You will take this path on your return). Continue to descend to a stone wall. Pass through the gate, keeping your dog on a lead or under close control, and descend on the worn path on the edge of a field. You will pass a shelter on your left. This was built in the late 19th century and was a grand kennel for fox hounds. After the barn, keep your dog on a lead or under close control and go through the kissing gate on your left. Continue descending on the edge of a field, with a stock fence on your right. On reaching the corner of the field put your dog on a lead and pass through the kissing gate. Continue on a path above the river and cross the stone bridge.

On reaching the quiet lane turn left. Pass a sports and social club on your left. On reaching the road, cross over and turn right. Continue on this road, where

you will reach a car park on your left and a large metal fingerpost. Turn right, cross the road and enter into Holland's Café. ❸

On leaving the café turn left. Continue on your outbound route. You will need to cross over to make use of the pavement. Turn left on reaching Shepard's Bridge Lane. Look for the waymarker on your right and cross the stone bridge. Continue on the footpath, where you will pass the shelter once again. Pass through the gate and continue to ascend between the bracken. On reaching a waymarker turn right. ❹ Now you leave your outbound route. Continue to ascend beside a stone wall on your right. Shortly after you will leave the stone wall. Cross over a plank, avoiding a wet area. Continue ascending between the bracken. On reaching a stone wall pass through a gate and enter into a plantation, where there are no livestock. Follow the path, which veers to your left and ascends steeply amongst the pine trees.

The path levels and you will pass through a gap in the stone wall. Here you leave the plantation and enter into oak woods. Continue on the obvious path, which is undulating to begin with and snakes through the wood. The path begins to descend and a little further you will see Coniston water on your right. Descend steeply and on reaching a stone wall pass through a small gate. Put your dog on a lead or under close control and descend on the obvious path, which cuts through the hillside. There are scattered mature trees throughout the landscape. On reaching a gate beside a stile, put your dog on a lead and pass through the gate. Turn left on a farm track. Follow the sign on the fingerpost for Low Yewdale. Ascend between the hedgerows, and shortly after turn right and pass through the farm gate. Keep your dog on a lead or under close control and continue straight ahead, ascend through the sloped field, following the obvious grass track.

Continue to ascend, where your views behind you extend over Coniston water. As you see estate fencing, follow the track, which bends sharply to your left. Continue through the farm gate and follow the worn track, which bends to your right. The grass track has a straight level section, where if you turn around you can have one last view over Coniston water.

The path ascends, and you will veer to your left. There are views to the fells ahead. Shortly after, veer right and continue on the track. You will reach a stone wall. Pass through the farm gate beside the stile. Continue straight ahead, ascending on the track between the hillocks. You will reach and continue beside a stock fence on your left. There is woodland beyond the fence. Near to the corner of the field you will reach a farm gate. Pass through the gate and continue straight ahead on the worn path through the middle of another hilly field. Head for the gable end of a building in the distance.

You will reach and pass through another farm gate. Now you are in a familiar spot. Tarn Hows cottage is straight ahead of you. Turn right on the tarmac path and retrace your steps. Just before reaching the road turn left and descend beside the stone wall on your left. Continue on this path, where you will reach back to your car.

16. Hawkshead

Medium - 4.8 mile - 2hr 30min

This fantastic circular walk starts in the forest. You will descend for much of the way, until reaching Hawkshead village. You can stop at the café 'Poppi Red', where there is seating inside or out. The walk back is not as taxing as you would think, as the ascent is much more gradual. You will pass through farmland, where on a clear day the views are fantastic. There may be livestock including cattle for parts of this walk. There are plenty of streams, where your dog can get a drink along the way.

How to get there – From Hawkshead village, continue on the B5285 and follow the sign for Coniston and Ambleside.
Turn left onto Hawkshead Hill (B5285), which is signposted for Coniston.

Grid Reference – SD 33174 98606

Parking – Free in the Forestry Commission High Cross car park

Cafe – Poppi-Red tel: 015394 36434

You will need – Dog lead, dog bags

Dog Friendly Tea Room & Café Walks - Lake District

The Walk

❶ From the car park, go to the furthest end away from the entrance, and ascend passed the vehicle barrier. Continue to ascend through the forest on the forest track, which has several short ascents along the way. As the main track bends sharply to your left you will see a footpath, ignore this and continue on the track following the sign for Hawkshead. Pass a stream on your left, where your dog can get water below the bank.

As you continue there is another stream on your left. Just after, ignore a track on your right. Continue straight ahead. Pass an area of broadleaved trees, which makes the area more open and light. Soon after there is a stream on your left, where your dog can get a drink. Just after, ignore a path on your right and continue around a left bend. Pass a mushroom carving on your right, and then a stream goes under your path.

On reaching another left bend, ignore the track on your right, and continue on the main forest track. Ignore a footpath on your left and just after, pass a cycle track on your right. You will have brief views on your left of the

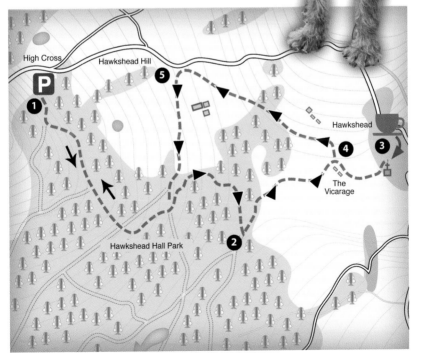

fells and Esthwaite water. Continue to descend. Just as you begin to descend you will reach a fingerpost. Turn left onto a bridleway, ❷ following the sign for Hawkshead. Descend on the path, with forest on your left and fields on your right. Cross a stream via the stones, and continue on the path between the bracken.

On reaching a farm gate pass through the kissing gate. Continue between the stone wall and a stock fence. You will see views ahead and houses. Put your dog on a lead here. Continue passed the houses on your right. Pass between grand gate posts and ignore the footpath on your left. Continue to the road and a fingerpost. Turn right, following the sign for Hawkshead via the church. Pass a lovely stone slab wall on your left, and a yew hedge on your right.

Continue through a gateway, where you will now have a stock fence on your left and a stone wall on your right. On reaching another gate, put your dog on a lead, or under close control and pass through the gate. Veer to your left, and cross the field. On reaching a fingerpost and gate, pass through the gate and continue straight ahead, beside a stone slab fence on the edge of a field. Pass through a gate into a cemetery and descend on the tarmac path.

On reaching the church, turn left and then take a narrow path on your right. Pass the front of the church. At the end of the church, turn left and then turn right. Pass through a gate and descend the steps. ❸ You will see Poppi Red café on your right. On leaving the café, turn left and ascend the steps back into the church grounds. Turn left, ignore the path on your right and pass the back of the church. Ignore paths on your left and right and continue straight ahead.

Ascend on the path to retrace your steps. Put your dog on a lead, or under close control and go through the gate. Continue on the field edge, and pass through another gate. Continue straight ahead and cross the field. Go through another gate and continue on the path, with the field on your right. On reaching the end of the path turn left, and soon after take the footpath on your right, following the sign for Tarn Hows and Coniston. ❹

Keep your dog on a lead or under close control, as there may be livestock. Pass through the kissing gate beside the grand gate post. Continue straight ahead (as if you had gone between the gate posts) and cross the field. Pass beside the mature trees on your left, and then on your right. You will see a gate ahead of you. Don't go through the gate but turn left, following the sign for Tarn Hows. Ascend on the edge of the field. Pass through a kissing gate and continue straight ahead, on a narrow path on the edge of a small field. Pass through another kissing gate at the end of the field, and beware of the electric fence on your right.

Continue straight ahead, on the edge of a small plantation. There are fields on your right and views to the fells beyond. Pass through another kissing gate and continue on the edge of the field, there is a stream below on your right. Pass through a copse of broadleaved trees. Your dog can get water as you cross a stream via a concrete slab. Take the rocky path ahead, but a little to your left. Ascend the steps and pass through a kissing gate, keeping your dog on a lead, or under close control. Cross through the middle of the field, where the views will remain on your right. Follow on the obvious worn path. You will pass a farmhouse on your far left. Cross a farm track and continue straight ahead. Descend, where you will reach close to the road. Don't go through the kissing gate on your right, but go through the small gate straight ahead. Keep your dog on a lead, or under close control. ❺ Turn left and follow the sign on the fingerpost for Grizedale Forest. Ascend beside the stream on your right, with a stone wall on your left. Continue beside the stone wall on the edge of the field. As you see a farm building ahead turn right and cross the field.

Pass through a gate and continue straight ahead. Cross over a hillock. The path isn't obvious, and is a little boggy. Continue ahead, where you will pass a telegraph pole. Pass a mature ash tree on your left, and then soon after you will pass mature sycamore trees. Head for a kissing gate at the end of the field. Pass through the kissing gate (it can be boggy here), and continue straight ahead, where just after, you will see a path on your left. A stream passes under the path. Ignore the narrow path on your left and continue straight ahead. The stream is on your right and you will see a forest ahead.

The grass path is only slightly worn, and again the area is boggy. You will see a wire fence, and the path veers to your right. Continue to a gate, and pass through it, where you will enter back into the forest. Continue to ascend gently on the narrow path. You will reach a familiar forest track. Turn right and ignore any paths or tracks on your left and right. Continue on this wide forest track, where you will retrace your steps back to the car park.

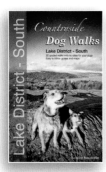

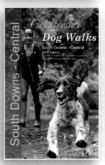

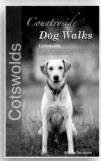

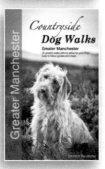